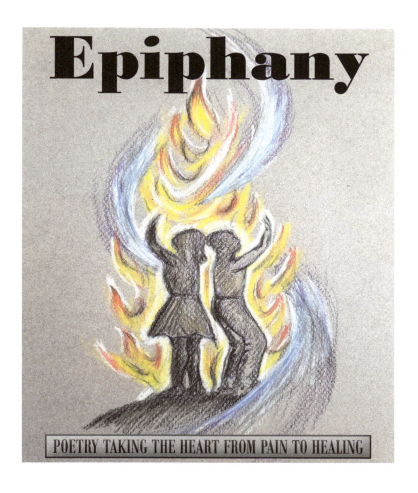

Title art by Kefee_the_artist from Atlanta, Georgia
Cover art inspired by Kefee_the_artist from Atlanta, Georgia

Tatianna Danielle and Alphonso Luciano

Copyright © 2022 Tatianna Danielle and Alphonso Luciano
All rights reserved
First Edition

NEWMAN SPRINGS PUBLISHING
320 Broad Street
Red Bank, NJ 07701

First originally published by Newman Springs Publishing 2022

ISBN 978-1-63881-375-0 (Paperback)
ISBN 978-1-63881-376-7 (Digital)

Printed in the United States of America

To our mother who was a victim of domestic violence. Rest in heaven, Stephanie Nicole.

Also, rest in heaven, Devon Adam. You are missed, little brother!

For those who have been victimized by the force of domestic violence, child abuse, or sexual assault, it invaded your life, family, and friends; it took the lives of the people you love, or you are a survivor putting the pieces of your life back together one day at a time.

For those dealing with mental health. Your days are filled with many thoughts, fears, and struggles each day. When you feel like no one cares or understands, take a moment to breathe. Seek help and guidance with any challenges you are experiencing. Please talk to someone.

For those wanting acceptance and love, but you cannot find it because of abandonment or rejection.

For those who are caught up in a situation, fearful of letting go because of violation of trust and care to your being.

For those who want safety and stability but continue to get caught up walking the same path, your struggles lay in your thoughts and actions, constantly straying in two different directions.

For those crying out in your actions and words. You yearn for someone to hear you, to take you seriously, but never heard.

This world is full of people who have the same or similar story. Someone feels the same as you. Though they remain voiceless, lingering in the shadows and feeling alone as if no one cares.

This poetry book brings thoughts of power and words that affect us physically and spiritually realigns. It allows our words to speak out loud. This poetry book is for ALL OF US!

Love and Peace,
—Tatianna Danielle and Alphonso Luciano

COMMUNITY RESOURCES

If you are immediate danger, call 911. For confidential help, 24/7, 365-day-a-year for individuals or families, please call the numbers listed.

National Child Abuse Hotline call 1-800-422-4453 (7233).

https://www.childhelp.org/hotline/

National Domestic Violence Hotline call 1-800-799-SAFE (7233).

https://ncadv.org/get-help

National Sexual Assault Hotline Call 1-800-656-HOPE (4673).

https://www.rainn.org/

SAMHSA'S National Helpline call 1-800-662-HELP (4357)

https://www.samhsa.gov/find-help/national-helpline

Poetry Reviews

Tatianna Danielle is a beautiful writer. Her poems make me feel a sense of validation and honor. Tatianna's poetry touches my heart, mind, and soul. After reading "Shattered" and "Beloved," I was empowered to face my heartache and pain.

—Q. Coachman

Alphonso Luciano poetry is real words being expressed and allows you to think about the words written. The poem "Such a Woman" is a visual and uplifting poem about a strong woman. It is very descriptive and allows you to open your imagination to see this woman in the light being displayed and takes you on a journey of a person you want to meet.

—M. Travis

Contents

Foreword 9
Acknowledgments 12
Introduction 15

Chapters

    Chapter 1:   Pain 17
    Chapter 2:   Strength 55
    Chapter 3:   Healing 83
    Chapter 4:   Love 101
    Chapter 5:   Peace 123

Written by Tatianna Danielle and
Alphonso Luciano 132

Foreword

As a dear friend of Tatianna Danielle, I was overflowing with excitement and was honored when she asked me to write the foreword to her and her brother's first poetry book. They are both incredible artists who have great talents to share with the world. My friendship with Tatianna began years ago when our families were stationed in Germany together. Tatianna Danielle and I are both (retired) military spouses who come from very humble beginnings; thus, our connection was seeded. Being a military wife drives you to proudly and strategically wear many hats as you support your active-duty military member. Let's just say overcoming troubled backgrounds coupled with military life drives you to be resilient real fast. Our friendship blossomed from a spiritual connection fashioning an amazing sisterhood.

There is no rainbow without rain. The reality is no one's journey is free from pain! When outsiders are looking in, many describe our lives by the successes that they see, looking only at the results and ignoring the rain that it took to get to the rainbow. To outsiders looking in, life may appear perfect and flawless, but remember that everyone experiences pain in one way or another. And the truth is, no matter who you are, how much money you have, where you live, or how famous you are, we all experience pain no matter our successes. Shame, fear, sadness, anger, and guilt are among the top painful emotions that humans experience.

Life is love. But life is also pain. Living life means experiencing emotional suffering as well as emotional bliss. Unfortunately, pain is an inevitable consequence of life, and we have to experience it whether we want to or not. As humans, we typically view pain as a negative experience, and understandably, we try to avoid it as much as possible. Pain can have a powerful hold on your mind, body, and spirit, so learning how to process and heal from it is crucial.

Tatianna Danielle and Alphonso Luciano have wrestled for many years to put their life's pain…hardships, traumas, healings, and joys into word on paper. It is no small feat to share your heart and hurt to the world and allow yourself to be vulnerable and share the painful truth that you have lived through with readers. This amazing act is a little, well…no, it's absolutely an amazing accomplishment! Tatianna Danielle and Alphonso Luciano have poured so much passion, wisdom, and emotion into these pages, and I am grateful for the profound encouragement and expression found in *Epiphany*.

I know and realize the magnitude that this book holds for Tatianna Danielle and Alphonso Luciano. The collaboration of raw vulnerable emotions *was* and *is* their truths—their story, their lives—in action. The art of expression is an amazing way to bring healing from pain. *Epiphany* is a series of poetic expressions, taking readers on a journey of living and processing pain. This poetry book captures that philosophy and guides readers on a genuine path that others can relate to during their own healing process.

The timing of *Epiphany* comes at a significant cultural moment as well as a time of distressful happenings in the world. In a society where we're pressured by voices both internal and external to suppress pain, it's inspirational to have a book of art that, in all its vulnerability, paves a road to processing healing. Healing in a healthy manner is imperative. With intentional hearts, Tatianna Danielle and Alphonso Luciano lead by example and will seize readers' attention by giving their authentic, melodic, heart-capturing poetry in *Epiphany*. This book is like a deep dive into years of pain and trauma and the road to healing.

One thing is for sure: this book will inspire you to begin or continue your own journey of healing life's pain. As it is artistically written, I can promise you that the situations and events reflected in these pages are raw unadulterated happenings, which will touch your life and remind you that "*you are not your pain.*"

> But let patience have its perfect work, that you may be perfect and complete, lacking nothing. (James 1:4 NKJV)

Love and light,
Wendy C. Wilson, PhD

Acknowledgments

Thank you to my brother for connecting with me on this project. Our collaboration is a piece of art. This time of writing has been a world of discoveries and a place for healing in my life. I could not have accomplished this without the determination and pushing you gave me; it truly allowed us both to touch the inner parts of our hearts for it to speak, hit rhymes, and hear songs only heard in the moments of writing. Visiting emotions and opening the soul to feel and forming them into words bring transparency for others to experience life and know that their imperfections are perfect in someone's eyes. We held each other's hands from afar, having times of laughter and moments of thinking about how we survived such things in our lives. With everything, I know the words written on paper will show others they can learn how to feel again and heal when the world writes you off and has no care for you as a person until you begin to speak and use your voice to tell your story through every corner your feet touched the earth. Take a moment to catch your breath; it is the most profound time after living in a survival mode most of your life. Open your eyes to clearly see yourself, understand the emotions felt, and truly begin to take the power back. We are in this together, and we can live without being shackled to another person's view of who we are to be. We can just be—free!

—Tatianna Danielle

Thank you to my striving sister for giving me a wonderful collaboration on this book. This was a big project considering all the things we have been through. I know it was hard to unveil our truths and open the door to emotions that were buried and face the secrets that were covered, hoping to not have to ever visit these corners in our lives. It has been a long time coming to state the least. As I reflect on the poems written, I think about the moments that defined me as the words in my poems defined so many others. Being able to create a story that is told through a series of words, my creativity took its place, uplifting me to a higher pinnacle in life. I am blessed to be the man I have become, finally being able to be that man I proclaim. I have visions of a brighter future even though I'm sitting here confined from society. My vision is now clearer; beneath me is the negativity, those who wish the worse for me. I stand in my stance, allowing my thoughts to transcend into these rhymes and riddles I use as a shield for everything that is formed against me, rising above my adversaries and being proud of myself and the miles I traveled to get here, maneuvering through the potholes of my everyday struggles, such as depression, loneliness, anxiety, and sleepless nights forming into a restless mood, confusion, and bitterness that swirl within my mind. I am just like you. Eyeing my surroundings, we are in this together. We are only deemed different through DNA. Your problems are the same as another. Two different stories but they are all the same. Different views but they are all the same. I recognize your pain, the blind eye we turn when faced with reality. We just cannot hide it; we cannot stay silent forever. The most beautiful sight at the end of any "Storm" is the colorful rays of a "Rainbow." Allow our words to reflect that same beauty. Life was never meant to be perfect, but it is said to be always worth it.

—Alphonso Luciano

To our tribe (my husband, all of our children, siblings, grandchildren, and closest friends), the light from you all really motivated us to want more out of life and to do better with ourselves, to give you all a better mother, a better father, a better sister, a better brother, a better aunt and uncle, and more importantly, a better person for the world to see. Being able to prevail over our enemies and the hate they give, you all are all amazing. With every word and expression written, you all helped us not give up when challenges came but to go even harder to allow God to use us for this time, formulating words that can only come from above. This poetry book is a start of our legacy and a footprint in this world; it is the birth of newness in our lives, and we are so glad to share this with you all. Thank you for all the support, long nights of readings, edits, and talks of how to get this to the world. We were told to make connections through this process, do our research, call everyone, and not give up until it was complete. You all are the greatest, and we are forever grateful for you all being in our lives.

With much appreciation, thank you.

Legacy is first started and then left to place a footprint in the world, not just a moment in time but work done that is remembered and touches people for years to come, being a voice that empowers and using words written to help people in their discovery, healing, and connections, just being a positive force in the world.

—Tatianna Danielle and Alphonso Luciano

Introduction

Epiphany is a collection of poems in which two siblings experienced moments of reawakening, touching the inner parts of their being to bring different emotions and feelings through life's circumstances, destruction of others, and decisions made using transparency to expose the heart of a person and show how there are so many things that bring pain in life. Still, peace can saturate the heart while forgiveness allows healing to free the whole person.

Every poem is written to take anyone reading on a journey to paint a picture from different perspectives in life and touch on different levels of pain experienced, such as abandonment, rejection, anger, trauma, loneliness, hopefulness, and forgiveness.

Take a moment to breathe, close your eyes to allow your mind to be able to not only see the words written on each page but to hear the rhythm and the path of the journey. Each poem is relatable to another person's story; if you find yourself feeling a connection or emotion, it is okay. Open your heart for your own journey of healing.

The poems will show how strength endures, peace, inner healing, and love gained through being hopeful in the encounters of each day's journey. As you begin and bring connections, you too will find moments of epiphany.

Chapter 1 - Pain

1.1 Without You by Tatianna Danielle 14
1.2 Emotions by Tatianna Danielle 18
1.3 Brokenness by Tatianna Danielle 19
1.4 The View by Tatianna Danielle 20

Epiphany

* Shattered by Tatianna Danielle 21
* Until I Breathe Again By Alphonso Luciano 25
* Anxiety by Tatianna Danielle 27
* Depression by Alphonso Luciano 30
* Alone by Tatianna Danielle 33
* Alone By Alphonso Luciano 35

1.5 Discouraged by Alphonso Luciano 38
1.6 Shadows by Alphonso Luciano 40
1.7 Overdose by Alphonso Luciano 41
1.8 A Touch by Alphonso Luciano 43
1.9 Apart… by Alphonso Luciano 45
2.0 Lonely by Alphonso Luciano 47

P<small>AIN</small>

Pain is a physical and emotional discomfort to the body causing hurt, torment, and suffering to every part of your being—a person will not experience true happiness until healing takes place.

—Tatianna Danielle

 Without You

Being in this world without you has left me with nothing but unanswered questions

Indescribable pain that I feel deep down in the corners of my soul

Sometimes I don't know which way to turn, I just don't know where to go

Feeling so many ways, so confused with these days

And in nights, these restless nights that come up occasionally have me tossing

Tossing and turning, reaching for you and screaming out your name

In the fogginess "mommy" I say

Thinking of your beautiful face and smile

While I lie in these endless tears that fall from my face

Dealing with disappointments by the people who are supposed to care

Has left me with more hurt than I can bear

I pause…who can I run to?

Being exposed to so many things, seeing these things I need some understanding

You see I'm lost, lost in these entanglements of lies wondering sometimes will I survive

I sit here, I see myself standing in the dark

Smoke screens cover my eyes you see, from getting away from the images I see

Perhaps standing in the middle of the street trying to figure out where I am supposed to be

Holding my head alone…in search, searching

While saying will this ever end?

You see you were the answer to every feeling, touch, and word that brings consolement to my being

However, you fade away before being able to reach me

Without you I'm lost, lost trying to put the pieces of my life together

While looking up to heaven for the answers to take away this pain others have cost

I tell you this roller coaster of life really has caused me pain

Spinning feeling bruised and violated

Every time the cycle of memories passes through my veins

I am determined to let these walls fall

Cultivating relationships, learning to trust, and raising my kids feel like a maze

I get caught up every time

Having to press through when seeing what you and others did

Man, having to explain to the counselors everything y'all did

I will always love you

Still, I get mad at times due to the destruction caused in my past

Like denying the truth, telling me I'm a liar when I said he touched because he did

Me wiping the blood off your back that he did

I even remember the day when you walked out

Darkness came over me

My heart was ripped out of me

I was left feeling empty at a tender age, and you never came back

By the way, I was <u>6</u> years old to be exact

In your absence dealing with getting beat by someone who saw you in me

Having a gun held up to my head thinking about death at the age of 16

Boy, I tell you these abuses by others has left images that are embedded in my brain

It has left me discombobulated in so many ways

Doing the opposite of how I was raised is best for me

Not wanting another generation to have to live with emotional struggles like I did

Still, every day a part of me hurts

Yearning for your love and affection, of a mother's touch

Yeah despite what you did and what happened to me I still need it

However, I realize I can sing any song to remind me of you

Look up to heaven to get a glimpse of you but I will forever be without you

I'm just left in this world without you.

Written by Tatianna Danielle

EMOTIONS

I am dealing with these emotions
Endlessly taking me on a journey
Telling me how my life used to be
Wrestling with these thoughts
that keep coming inside my head
The ups and downs
The cloudiness of life
Every emotion trying to consume me
and take the best of my life
Lord why me?
Why does double-mindedness keep
wanting to creep up in my head?
Why do I keep tossing and turning in this bed?
Why are these images causing me to be scared?
Why do these emotions cause these tears?
Rolling down like rain
Waiting for these emotions to end
Looking to see sunshine in my day

Written by Tatianna Danielle

Brokenness

Brokenness has drained my heart
shattered my inner being from productivity being seen in all its days
torn into so many pieces, no one will stay
multilayered levels of brokenness, no one is immune
no trust lives in this space, so people are pushed away
toiling for hours with thoughts of deceit, while the clock continues to turn each hour
lost in time, while others continue their day
meticulous destruction that has no name
just continues to break others repeatedly, there is no end
mirrored images plague my mind, of what has happened over time
stuck in the middle of reality and dishonesty, not sure how the two can meet
seems like a mistake, still the reason remains unclear
is there a way to recover, to retract all the wrongdoings?
take back everything from the past
can the brokenness be healed and the mistakes that pierced my being be corrected so I can live freely?
a living soul to be captured, take my hand and forgive
walk with me to clear this path to allow brokenness to end

Written by Tatianna Danielle

The View

From these streets I see lies, hurt, and confusion that have taken the lives of the innocent
It's like one door opens to reveal the next and the next deceit of another
The person standing in the middle is hit with blows wondering how to surrender.
I can't explain the cycle of torn hearts and blood shed
All I know is these endless thoughts of abandonment and rejection plague my head.
The reality to find peace is like…
Flashbacks of mirrored images effects hoping one day to find that eternity of peace.
I know someone told me to let it go, to move on
But how when all you see is a generational cycle that continues to play itself
over, over, and over again in my head
No one is willing to take the stand with you to bring resolve
It's like standing alone in a room screaming for your voice to be heard
For the pain to be removed and for someone to hold you
Telling you the nightmare is only in your dreams
How can this be when it is all I see? It's really my reality.

Written by Tatianna Danielle

Shattered

I stand in this place of numbness
As the tears fall down my face
I don't know if I can move
if I am breathing
my heart has just taken a beating
crushed and dismantled into pieces
that may not ever be connected
I feel stuck waiting for the deceit
and violation to be removed
I want to be woken up from this dream
Oh! This really just happened to me
Now faced with the reality, I am
disappointed and angered
It is hard for me to explain this pain
should I scream hoping it will release the pain
that is settling in the core of my being
Oh, God! It came so unexpectantly on
a day that you created for me
We were supposed to be celebrating,
laughing, and enjoying the time

But what I feel is devastation, shattered by
what has just been revealed to me
I don't know why you would treat me this way
Why couldn't you have just talked to me
I've given you nothing but purity and loyalty
Making sure you were my priority
exposing myself through transparency,
I have been clear from the start
committed to our dreams but you just made it
clear you don't care, is this beyond repair
I may have hurt you, but this is not fair
I can't erase the past but I can spend time to
acknowledge fear brought emotions that were released
through the tongue and my apologies for every time
they landed on your heart, it was never intended to
tear you apart, so please forgive me for my part
The brutal treatment and verbally
abusing me was never in our plan
Our goal was to ride this thing out enjoying
every moment hand in hand
You were my soulmate, enjoying our love
However, you have transformed into this person,
I don't understand and I can't see the man who

shared all these plans with me, I cannot see the
newness you claim to be due to the darkness
that surrounds the purity in your soul
So, I am left alone fighting for what we are to be
but suffocated by all the things you have done to me.

I am staying strong, but you have to
stop blaming this all on me
I am shattered in every part of my being
waiting for relief to rescue me
I need security and safety, bringing back
the loyalty and trust, respect and care
Can you give that to me? Do you care?
Shattered in my reality, while wishing
we could make amends
Shattered waiting for these moments to end
I want to go back to respect and honesty,
tranquility, just consistency
I want to go back to the love we
share, for the rest of our days

Shattered by this reality

Written by Tatianna Danielle

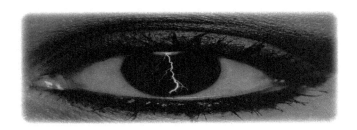

Until I Breathe Again

I never thought I would experience this
imagine hearing such words
my heart became broken, my speech was torn
I just couldn't breathe
a tear welled up beneath my eyelids
my vision instantly obscured
I shivered chillingly
to think you could even say those words to me touched
me unspeakably, it opened an unhealed wound
like pouring salt on a wound that never has healed
I was shocked, baffled, and suddenly amazed
saddened and disturbed—in a daze
scuffled in my mind, shuffled in time
seconds moved slow, my head hung low
my chin tucked to my chest
I could just scream, shout, holler
I just wanted to yell and fight but was crippled instead
I spoke the harshness of words that came to my head
I hated you, I hated myself even more
I couldn't believe you, I believed in you
I tried to give you the best of me
I just wanted you to love me
I tried to relate, but as I saw it was too late
it was just a feeling that caused my
knees to buckle like what?
I was frozen in a moment
my mind went blank

actually I did have one thought
"How does a mother turn her son
against his own father?"
my soul diminished, my temper flared ready to spit fire
"What did I do to deserve this?"
you my flesh, my blood, my son…my family
I knew that wasn't you speaking
I knew that ain't how you felt
but "How does it feel?"
my hands clasped to my face
stagnant in place, my emotions soared
a frown wrinkled my complexion
my expression was beyond explanation
I look at you and see me all in your features
my son…every man's destiny
that boy to carry on his father's legacy
incarcerated the agony is real
my pain is more real, my reality is like a thriller
my palms sweaty, heart beating crazy
my breathing unsteady
"until I breathe again"

By Alphonso Luciano

ANXIETY

I have these feelings that suddenly
affect my whole mental state
I am not able to describe to anyone what is taking place
It can come at any time, without notice
Triggered depending on environmental constraints
Different levels of severity depending
on the person or place
overwhelming thoughts consume me,
mixed signals or false in its nature
ongoing images and situations that will not stop
So many thoughts running all through my head
Disrupting the core of my soul, being attacked
My heart begins racing, pulsating
I am in fight or flight with no recollection of my being
I feel like I cannot breathe, as my
lungs seem to suffocate me
I want to hide in a corner, lock myself in
the room until these feelings end
But I am stuck where I stand
I feel numb and cannot gather my thoughts

My eyes begin to strain, so I cannot see
My heart is sinking; I just want to
run away with the wind
But I am weak and scared to be seen
in such a vulnerable state
I want to hide in a place where I am
unexposed to this world, we live in
the cruelty of people's judgment but
never offers a helping hand
I don't want outbursts to damage the people
close to me; eruptions shaking our foundation
They must not see the explosions, fire
ignited intensely coming out of me
I am fearful of the dark moments
that are not remembered
I don't want anyone to see this anxiety
I am searching for healing—God,
please do not let this kill me
I pray the tears will end; I want to
have normalcy in my day
Anxiety you have to leave today.

Written by Tatianna Danielle

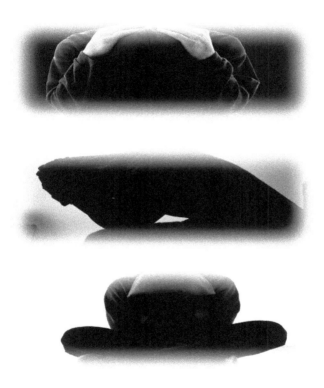

Depression

It's hard to be me.

even I can't stand in front of the mirror and take in the image before me.

dwelling for a moment on the man I become, spiritually hung.

seeing the tears forming over my aging features take me by surprise, and it's always the question why.

sleepless nights transcend in a foggy haze. to the days I'm just wandering in a stormy daze.

Depressed, thinking it's all in my age

so confused in my stubborn ways, ignoring the signs of a problematic phase

feeling like I'm suffering, lost in a mental maze.

Just thinking it's all a figment of my imagination

Simply closing my eyes to the truth, just to realize.

"My depression is a problem to you."

the tossing and turning in my sheets, perspiration in my sleep

"Do you even have a clue?"

what I go through from bullet wounds through and through.

irritated mood to feeling alone, and rude.

The distance in my head, laying on a metal slab wanting to escape the voices in my head

Eye shifting from a brick wall to pictures of my loved ones, this darkness is real; it has me contemplating with the dead.

deep regret inhaled like a cigarette, exhaled by pain slowly tearing me apart

as an adolescent facing neglect, as a teen feeling like a reject. Assumptions of failure befuddle my thoughts. Too many words to define.

many years jailed and confined, shackled to the ways of past times

these racing thoughts that play back and forth causing all hell in my mind

disturbance of suicide awakens my sleep periodically. Spazzing in my head automatically

Pleading on my knees, drowning in despair drastically

I need to breathe, please, weeping in fear these tears seem like moments of dying on the inside within a place somewhere to hide. To hear my story, you would think I was lying against this depression, within a place somewhere in the back of my mind, it's hard to even tell.

misled, lost, and not knowing if this will ever end

I want this depression to detach itself from me, stop being misleading
I want to be confidently posed, instead of being suddenly imposed upon by violations you bring to my thoughts paralyzing my body and oppression trying to control my every thought and movement synchronized with your time, I wonder how this all came upon my life so suddenly still, I crumble, my thoughts continue to be like an endless tunnel.
I pop these pills trying to fight the urges, not wanting to deal with the exposure of this depression
They think something is just wrong with me, but never thought this depression is beyond my ability
it is too complicated, beyond my ability to articulate, and discouraging to say the least
This depression is greedy; my mental state is the ultimate feast begging in agony to detach itself from this leash.
however, I have to maintain the fighting emerging beast
my depression, I suppose a deep regret, it has no understanding
I lay here suffering; no one cares about this depression that disrupts my being.

Written by Alphonso Luciano

Alone

Alone in my room I keep staring at this wall
And in the back of my mind I keep
asking myself how did I fall?

Broken and dismayed by this person
who once knew my name
Moments of hearing the words
"stay, don't leave, don't go"
Now there is not even a whisper to show you are near
Only emptiness around

From loveliness to brokenness
Verbally attacking
Just pulling me down

Blows to my side; no one is around
Distrust and loneliness, darkness and shame
Emotional breakdowns, depression and pain
Bruised and scared soul; just let me go

It's not my fault; I'm not the one to blame
Do you understand it can't continue this way?
A steel wall for safety, never a white picket fence
Disconnection from the world—it doesn't make sense

Do you hear me calling your name?
What happened to the love once shared
The exchanged energy of respect and care?
Now numbness consumes me
Alone no one cares

Written by Tatianna Danielle

Alone

I don't know much about much, but I
have learned a lot about a lot.
I sit here thinking about my life as I remember it to be.
The late nights and the early mornings.
The days I would feel like something was
different, feeling like I was different.
That's when I noticed the change in my
behavior, I noticed the act in my actions,
the missing link between me and acceptance.
The fainthearted in being alive, the weak in being alive.
I just write, writing down all my struggles,
all my fears, believing one day I will be set free.
Free from these razor wire fences,
free in my mind to accomplish
whatever I put my mind to.
In a sense I'm like a loner, I don't have any
friends, I don't get along with others; considered
to be standoffish, quiet and weird.
Disqualified, so I can only shrug my
shoulders and say "so be it."

But my aim is high; my whole life
people told me I couldn't do it.
I wanted to play football, but I always
heard that I was too small.
I used to want to box, but I wasn't bold enough.
I used to draw, but that wasn't my passion.
I picked up on cutting hair, but I
didn't have the patience.
I've been searching for my purpose,
but I just can't seem to find it.
I've never even been in love, though there were
plenty of girls that captivated my interest.
I always seemed to push them away.
I was insecure. I had trust issues and abandonment issues.
I was dealing with situations that unfortunately
led me to drugs and alcohol.
I don't know. I'm just venting.
Hoping someone out there won't mind listening.
I really don't have anybody else to talk to.
So, I relied on my pencil and paper—you
see it gets me by in times like this.
Those dark moments when I'm alone and anxious,

When I feel like don't nobody love me, it's that moment when depression takes over. When I'm just down, wanting to cry, my body aching, my head throbbing. I'm thinking too much, thoughts are overwhelming, and I look around—nobody is there. There to hold me, talk to me, or just to give me that comfort from the look of their eyes. Warmth doesn't seem to exist, just a cold chill from my past. Tossing me from side to side in my sleep. My vision is deep, knee deep, like bending knees when I pray for forgiveness. I urge, seeking for a helping hand, leaping for faith. I'm just a man. Hopeless in my hope, my ill brother died shooting dope. Found with the needle still in his arm, my mind flickers, I'm still bearing arms. My story told through tattooed arms. Smiling like a charm but ain't nothing funny. Alarming I was living in harm, weeds flourishing like a farm.
"Alone."

Written By Alphonso Luciano

Discouraged

I'm ready to leave, it's so hard to believe
I'm putting my family behind me
I said a prayer, it's all behind me
Digging deep into my layer, in my element like a player
I made my peace with God at least
Passing out peacefully, it's over
Gracefully that fast, simply, finally at last
Looking sleepy, deeply—What was I thinking?
One could only imagine feeling alone and harassed
Bullied and clashed, seeing the whispering and heckling
Hearing the jokes and laughter, the stares and glares
Finger-pointing and dares
Sensing the cruel paranoia
Feeling like an oddball, a weirdo to mention a few
They call me the worse of names
There were the ruthless of games
Discouraged, nobody listening
Nor cared to pay attention—Now I am missing
It feels like it was destined
End it all was my only resolution; I
was trying to find a solution
Trying to be mutual, but it was crucial
They just ignored me, pushing me aside
Curled up at my bedside, knees tucked to my chest
My defense mechanism at best
Scared and frightened
Never mind my concerns

Stuck in a room all day, stalled away
Fearful of society and what it made me
Barely even eating, my heart barely even beating
They just ignored me…I wonder
if they hearing me now?
I hated myself
They never noticed the cuts and scars
Not my faintness and bruises
I was screaming, mentally abusing
Yelling to release me from such distress and confusion
From the things I endured
I can't take it no more
From those before
Those who alienated me forced me to throttle
At the break of no tomorrow
Now it's just an empty pill bottle
I wonder if they hear me now…discouraged

Written by Alphonso Luciano

Shadows

I walk thru the shadows
my thoughts are quite shallow
my movement is mellow
just as my speech
I softly shuffle my feet
thru the shadows—I walk
just me and my thoughts
my heart paces to an odd beat
a feeling of abnormalities
I chase familiarities within myself in all actuality
I can't seem to find it; there are no similarities
I'm lost and hopeless, yet fearless
my mind is cloudy while my actions speak loudly
I'm a mess holding on but I want to let go of this pain
to the hurt and loneliness
I don't want to embrace a sense of phoniness
wanting to laugh rather than cry
I'm trying to escape the thoughts in my mind
I can't help but to inquire
all these thoughts have me crying—my eyes dry
I walk thru the shadows, my thoughts are quite shallow
my movement is mellow, just as my speech
I softly shuffle my feet thru the shadows
I walk just me and my thoughts

Written by Alphonso Luciano

Overdose

everything went black.
I just want to get it back.
to everything that's lack.
even to those who slack.
my complexion pale.
I'm cold, and numb.
slowly I'm fading.
I no longer even have a pulse.
from these pills I tossed.
foam expelling from my mouth
even my nose.
cutting off my circulation with this hose.
this high got me feeling bossy.
my eyes glossy.
I'm not even thinking.
nor blinking.
I'm dying.
as they compress on my chest.
I can't remember a thing.
to even how I got here.
lying on the ground.
hunched over the steering wheel.
submerged in a bathtub.
collapsed on the floor.
bodies sprawled out at the door.
the blast was so electrifying.
my outcome terrifying.

I'm ruining myself.
my family looking at me.
baffled.
like, look at yourself.
I'm ashamed.
I'm a mess.
I can't face it.
results of being a failure.
giving up on so much.
it's so touching.
to gain so little.
life so belittling.
fighting this addiction.
RIP "Li'l Bro"
"overdose"

                Written by Alphonso Luciano

A Touch

why must we talk about it?
you were supposed to be here
right here, a lover and a friend who understands
living thru fear; I feel like I am always gasping for air
as it seeps from the tier, or just someone to care
for me to depend on, now I feel walked on
distracted from the world
sensationally wrecked, collided, needing a guide
in my mind where I hide
just from a single touch
I rush, almost seeming like it's never enough
the dreams in my head are crushed by falling stones at the highest lust
for attraction and attention
I thrive for a longing drive
I derive from a darker place
look at the pain in my face
I'm not supposed to be here
terrified.
upon my past.
my nights were verified
sleepless and restless
my outcome was solidified
walking amidst my burdens
of wrongdoings
and being wrongly accused.
verbally abused.

mentally excused.
and exhausted.
just from a touch.
the feel of a rush.
the voices that become hush.
shoulders that brush.
amongst one another.
like elbow to elbow.
blow to blow.
from my highs to lows.
ultimately below.
I'm faced with my life from beyond and above.
…"A Touch"…

       Written by Alphonso Luciano

Apart...

why you keep saying that?
why you keep acting like that?
it's like you keep trying me.
your attitude is pushing me.
pushing me further away.
I'm trying to stay.
I wanna stay.
I just love how your hips sway.
we been doing this for way too long.
"What's wrong?"
it seems as if you ain't feeling me.
you ain't doing the things you used to.
back and forth arguing.
this is getting old.
your side of the bed is getting cold.
you was just my baby, my girly, this isn't fair.
our future was planned and plotted.
despite all the cheating and lying.
all that childish talk.
tempers flaring, doors slamming.
lips spitting venom fuming like a chimney.
I still love you, just as you love me.
I just don't understand.
I'm feeling different.
it's awkward.
even over bacon and grits the conversation isn't the same.
your perfume even changed.

you tearing me apart.
we pose to be in love.
this ain't adding up.
how did this start?
where do we go?
rewinding the hands of time.
long walks in the park.
late-night lovemaking.
kisses staring up at the moon.
kids sneaking out after dark.
humping and grinding.
writing love letters.
100% Ginuwine playing in the background.
thinking about you, missing you.
my heart would flutter.
…you tearing me apart…

        Written by Alphonso Luciano

Lonely

I gaze at your images
hanging from my wall.
a stone wall.
a lonely wall.
a cold wall.
I stare at it often.
my mind shifts from
thought to thought.
relentlessly.
often I think about
the loneliness.
I ponder upon the
pain, and turmoil.
the restless nights.
the dosing in and out
of consciousness.
but I see you, and
manage to smile.
a smirk of a smile.
knowing that you are there.
not really, but you are.
in my mind you take me
above, and beyond.
I'm able to think far.
further than ever before.
the gleam was spectacular.
I seemed cornered.
overwhelmed.
the depression was thick.
missing you was like
a missing piece.
my fingers severed
into tiny pieces.
I felt deleted.
forgotten.
as time spent aimlessly.
my thoughts vividly.
endless despair.
but it's your beauty
that I see.
that motivates my spirit.
my soul yearns for the
sound of your voice.
the tender touch
of your reach.
but I'm behind this wall.
a stone wall.
a lonely wall.
a cold wall.
I stare at it often.
as it seems to stare
back at me.
haunting me.

sparing me from
all my fears.
concealing all my tears.
I face it, hoping,
and wishing.
voices mumble
through the night.
the air stale and congested.
down and depressed
just me, myself, and I.
needing you, wanting you.
I just dream.
lonely in my skin.
in this world confused
and bothered.
"Lonely"

Written by Alphonso Luciano

Chapter 2 - Strength

2.1 The Storm by Tatianna Danielle 52
2.2 Beautiful by Tatianna Danielle 53
2.3 The Truth by Tatianna Danielle 54
2.4 Purpose by Tatianna Danielle 58

Epiphany

* The Art of Me by Tatianna Danielle 60
* The Art of Me by Alphonso Luciano 63
* Superwoman by Tatianna Danielle 66
* Such a Woman by Alphonso Luciano 68

2.5 Strength by Alphonso Luciano 70
2.6 Pressure by Alphonso Luciano 71
2.7 Sometimes By Alphonso Luciano 72
2.8 My Mind by Alphonso Luciano 74
2.9 Life by Alphonso Luciano 76

STRENGTH

Strength is endurance during the most difficult circumstances in a person's life; broken and torn, yet you stand, lost and confused about how the day will end and even when you think you're falling apart you still stand. Strength comes to reassure you that you have the courage to continue, you have the strength to go through the storm, you have strength to change directions to keep moving forward.

—Tatianna Danielle

The Storm

In the midst of a storm, I can count on
strength to roar like a lion from the inside
pouring out the elements needed to survive the storm
connecting to the earth, opening heaven
to develop the resilient self to impact the
blow at the highest speed needed
to defeat the giant standing in the path of victory
strength is needed at the moment
when I have no one to rely on
no one to call
when lost, it is the first defense
it has to get me through the trenches
The corners that are hard to pass
it is all I have
I call on strength to touch the weakest bone
cause it to rise
to pull me through in the midst of time
to move quickly until my soul is satisfied
strength stops the winds from blowing
calms the noises around
removes the fears that are within
strength is my grip
It tightens with its intensity
Carries me until I reach dry land

Written by Tatianna Danielle

BEAUTIFUL

Hey, beautiful…
I see you command the room as you arrive
everything stops for a moment in time
not noticing you are very rare
the presence of you is quite unique
so divine, a perfect jewel
mesmerized by your beautiful light
illuminated for all to see the beauty within you
unable to blink, such a beautiful sight
your eyes soft and calm
eloquently opening your soul to the world
your smile lightens your face and paints a picture of hue
you are easily connected with everyone in the room
you allow your guard to be down, to voice your concern
open and vulnerable
a majestic movement that makes others sigh
you're transparent in every stride
to show that you are doing good on the surface
hair flowy, makeup on point, clothes proportioned
just a good look
as the day ends and you say your goodbyes
hey, beautiful, did you live today, or did you survive?

Written by Tatianna Danielle

The Truth

The truth is…
The truth is, I spent many years questioning every thought
Every step to please the person on the other side
Put how I felt inside on hold, covered up the hurt and smiled
Bent over backward for anyone to tell me I was accepted
Looked for love in all the wrong directions
Wanted the one closest to me to give approval, love from you, to be accepted
Not sure the agreement you and my mother had, but I felt rejected
Causing for rejection to be seen on every corner I turned on this earth
Insecurities held me back, shackled me from being the true me,
Caused me to be fearful of everything, lost in a world of someone else's pain
I want to be free; I just want to walk in truth

The truth is, so much stuff has happened in my life; it's sometimes hard to talk about
More losses than gains, disappointments and violations have left a whole lot of pain

People don't understand and think something is wrong with me
Having to defend everything, people think I am lying when I say this happened to me
Scared to expose the people, so I walked the streets feeling alone,
having no one to call, no one on my side to have my back at any time

So I had to learn to be on my own and make moves beneficial for me
I have asked myself why this world is so cold, even when the sun shines
In desperation I put my hands up, look to the sky while I cry, asking the Lord why
Is this pain I feel the blame for how I feel each day
The rejection of people will continue to push me in a corner and not allow the world to know the true me; I just want to walk in truth

The truth is, I don't want to close the door every night, sit in this pain I feel in my heart
I want to be rescued from every thought and feeling of rejection
I want to be accepted for who I am

All the scars that are in the process of healing, I want to expose for a brighter day
I don't want to place a mask over the feelings to continue to disrupt my days

The birthmark of pain, show sadness on my face
No judgment in doing so, I just want to walk in truth

The truth is, destruction by others almost killed me
Instead of dying while smiling
I approached the world through the eyes of determination
Allowing strength to be used in every situation

Not giving up when storms came, but pushing through no matter how many times I fell
Held my head up, always watched my steps and tracked every move
Didn't allow pride or shame to keep me from walking these streets, I just want to walk in truth

The truth is, I am doing what I can to be who I am
I apologize if I have done anything that may have caused destruction to your path
So many messed up thoughts, trust issues have interrupted my process
But I am back now, had many days of therapy to help me cope with my realities
Not to say I don't have challenges in my days, can't erase what has been done to me
All I ask is to be accepted for who I am; don't tear me down. I just want to walk in truth

Written by Tatianna Danielle

PURPOSE

Your purpose drives you to be anything you want to be
So why do we allow others to determine our destiny
No this cannot be, you have to take control of the things that you desire to be

Not letting the opinions of this world to change your thoughts
It is not about what they see
It is all that was imparted by your mother before you were to be
birthed into this world for all to see you unfold
like a butterfly you awoke, you made your sound heard within minutes of entrance
as time continues you explored every corner of the environment to get you to where you can spread your wings and fly alone on this earth
in the nick of time, you will be making decisions that shape your being
on a road to having everything you dreamed of and making them reality

your purpose will be seen through your feet treading the world with the strength you were able to build from the obstacles that blocked you and made you fail
however, you did not allow things to keep you down
you picked up the pieces and got up off the ground
your purpose will keep you in the game of life
you can be whoever you want to be
it is important you understand that others cannot shape this reality
God gave you the tools to be
Allow your purpose to drive you in every way

                Written by Tatianna Danielle

THE ART OF ME

I was formed to be this way
Painted on the brick walls
With a blank stare
Shocked by the world's rhythm
In a state looking tender and fragile
Embracing individuals, thinking this would be fine
Just not knowing the thoughts of another, can get you every time
Looking for love in the touch
While the voice captivates with the tone that wasn't rough
Soothing the touch of all human beings, just don't violate me

I was groomed to be polite, say yes ma'ma and yes sir
And to not look a person in the eyes when they speak is considered rude
And don't even think about talking back with that tongue, keep it closed at all costs
But listen intensely taking notes of every word, movement, and thought
Survey the room, know the point of every entrance
And exit when things don't look right in my mind, just pay attention
Leave without anyone noticing you were even in the room

The silent person in the corner
Do you see me on your wall?
A painted picture of curiosity and beauty

Stopping you in your tracks and you wonder why this is to be
Taking key of everything
Know when to make a chest move, like I am competing in a game
Follow the birds because they know when to turn directions when someone comes in the room
When the seasons change the silence in the air
allows you to follow the wind, ride on its back you will be glad you did

When threat appears at your doorstep
Run as fast as you can or fight to win
It is the respect in the streets, still the corruption bothers me
Loyalty being corrupted by the people you trust
So you kept your eyes open to not get stuck
In the ways of another man, cannot be
Build your name to be remembered
Being dignified when you walk the streets
Survival is your everything
This is the art of being me

    Written by Tatianna Danielle

THE ART OF ME

This is the art of being me, fighting to be free.
The numbness of running in place until my toes bleed.
To dream is to know what it means. Or is it all just a fantasy?
Burying these images in the back of my mind. Deep-rooted in time.
From long ago urging these feelings that's hard to ever let go.
This is me, the man I proclaim to be.

Masterpieces derive in my heart.
Overwhelming abnormalities.
Bristles softly define the canvas of these strange faces, appearing within these strange places.
When you look in my eyes, the dark stare penetrates, reflecting my soul.
A glare of emptiness rather a glimpse that grows fonder by the urge to take strides that leave others behind.
Black is beauty, it is seen through the light of night, like a neon glow.

This is the art of being me, intrigued by the young man that stood in front of me.
Strong and ambitious I try to be.
Relentless in my words, unsettling train of thought slightly disturbed.
This is me described with every verb.
I heard every name on the curb, misconstrued they even called me a nerd.

To baffle a crook, hide the truth, put it in a book. Grasping attention like bait on a hook.
Scared of success, we fear what we don't understand.
I gave it my all, put everything behind me I was never shook.
Chest pieces on the board, always two steps ahead.
Trying to figure me out, captivated by the voices in my head.
Opportunity in my next move, think strategically, plan accordingly.

The art of being me, a warrior, talking with precision.
Walking amongst the shadows fumbling with these decisions.
The most powerful force is the universe.
It's the silent power, to focus your thought like a leaning tower.
Mental penetration, calm, and powerful concentration.

It's the art of being me, actualized by the intelligent use of direction.
In sync with the environment that surrounds me.
Overcome many enemies that lurk where my feet have tread.
Or maybe it's just my (perception of what I heard) conception.
Part one to this is an inseparable relation.
A woman designed of a large magnitude, my sister such a wonderful collaboration.
With life we get two choices one is an amazing celebration, the other leaves devastation.
This is the art of me.

Written by Alphonso Luciano

Superwoman

I wake in the morning to check out the woman that I am
I unfold my body like a butterfly preparing to spread my wings
I stretch every limb to wake up my inside
Thank God for the day before my feet hit the ground
Gain enough energy to get out the bed, to walk the path of discovery

I approach the mirror, so we become one…me, myself, and I
My eyes lock with the woman I see on the other side
I look at myself, every flaw is seen
In this mirror, I don't know if I like what I see
Some days I am prettier than other days
I thought I liked the woman in me
But my self-esteem is making me question the me I see
I feel like I must change to fit the images seen
A world of critical judgments, stereotypes, and bias… but why

The world will let you know your flaws
When you don't measure up to the woman on the other side
You begin to tell yourself I wish I had her body
Her hair is beautiful, long and sleek, short and free, curly or straight
That woman is prettier than me
I don't like the me I see

Skin tones, hair texture, body type…why does it matter
People tell you to change to fit the image seen
Because of this I am lost trying to figure out how I am supposed to be
In my sight, I am left with questions like what do I wear, how do I walk, are those heels the right size, will this outfit Cause for someone to say something negative about me today
I am always feeling the need to change because that is what the world is saying I have to be.

                Written by Tatianna Danielle

Such a Woman

A woman strong and irresistible
unproblematic and flexible and suitable
a woman of beauty and integrity
a woman of any man's desire
great personality with a strong mentality
variously driven, you are giving
like a colorful butterfly upstream
an artistic dream full of grace
your characteristics cannot be traced
wishing for your embrace
just imagining your face
such a woman
you can't be replaced
I yearn for your tenderness
wonderfulness leads to your touch of elegance
excellence is seen in all you do
in your demeanor you are flawless
while society continues to be much meaner
thicker than leaner

no comparison, just a sincere soul
opening the heart to the unknown
such a woman
to endure pureness is a gift unexplained
the ultimate flow of your presence is unspeakable
assures fascination and dedication to
be you each and every day
every sense of aspiration
such a lady or rather should I say
…"such a woman"…

Written by Alphonso Luciano

Strength

Strength is bold.
strength can be cold.
strength knows neither young or old.
strength is where you remain firm; never fold.
firm in your approach, strong to the touch.
strength is focus, moving silent and stern.
motion upon the surface.
fists brutalize the structure of humankind.
smiles form into frowns.
strength overwhelms the force of doubt.
doubt sides with uncertainty.
strength is sincerity in means of prosperity.
strength can be a weapon.
not formed unbearable.
strength is unbreakable, remarkable.
strength of a nation is strength of our people.
strength of the gods.
strength is me.
strength is you.
strength is defined by the foundation you build,
by the energy put into the atmosphere.
strength is strong, it stands with a purpose.
strength is mental.
it's beyond physical, more than typical.
strength is not just an action, further than just a feeling.
strength unites.
strength creates love.
it's a blinding sense to the fact.
to the fact that we all have the ability to be strong.
strength is in us all.
strength is universal.
"Strength"

Written by Alphonso Luciano

Pressure

Pressure is what lies beneath the surface
it's a feeling that is seen upon your face
forever shifting from place to place
it's deep and absolute
like pressure thru a flute
the air traveling from your lungs
the pressure beneath your feet
either to do or not to do
it's confusing but causes you to choose
choosing between what is right and what is wrong
it's neither winning or losing
it's compelling
pressure is a measure, measuring the distance of each step
taking the time to think of everything in an instance
pressure can be that voice in the back of your mind
that tick in your brain that will define
the next move and turn
allowing the pain in your eye to
release the tale in your lies
it's indecisive and apprehensive
untamed in so many ways
like a beast in the wild
the forgotten child
it sounds in the night as a hurling howl
…"pressure"…

Written by Alphonso Luciano

Sometimes

sometimes I'd rather not be here
amongst the agony
amongst the misery
amongst the hate
everything recycling with time
second thoughts to articulate
a moment to formulate
locked away in a cold world
pushed away but still I stay
sometimes…
I'd rather not be here
standing with my back to the wall
I look down wanting to fall
broken from my downward spiral
I sometimes just wanna end it all
this is my call
ain't nobody hearing me, it's like they are ignoring me
sometimes…
I'd rather not be here far away, dim no gleam
so it may seem unbalanced like a beam
the force of a team
I hear the voices screaming in my head
shouting Do it! go ahead
it seems nearly impossible
but I stay, wanting to leave
needing to flee
my spirit so sunken this can't be

sometimes…
I'd rather not be here
this can't be living from a heart so giving
"look around you!"
it's unbearable
unpleasant, unmanageable
I pray for a difference
it feels unforgivable
I'm cursed
haunted
my eyelids slowly closing
I'm losing
I'm afraid
… sometimes…

Written By Alphonso Luciano

My Mind

I am in my mind just thinking
it's funny how people tend to judge you
and they don't even know you
or sometimes they know you but just envy you
behind my back I hear the chatter
and the fraudulent laughter
then in my face smiling
I peep at the snake in disguise
I knew the story before the end
"Why play me close?"
when it's just all for pretend
I sense the betrayal and even the malice you intend
I stand alone in my mind just thinking
there's no reason, it's the same thing every season
words can be so devastating
I'm just stating
loyalty can be mistaken but to love
me on these terms is faking
my heart aching…I can't take it

"Why even hug me?"
don't embrace me, just leave me be
in my mind it's like wasted time
it's defined with uncertainty
in all this movement I must decline
friendships declared and denied
in my mind described as war
my thoughts from afar to hate me is what they adore
my tears drop to the floor on and on like an encore
I've been here before
in my mind, where nothing truly exists
just my thoughts, another dimension outside from here
in my mind...

Written by Alphonso Luciano

LIFE

A standstill in time
it moves slow, slow as the thoughts in your mind
as the pain in your veins, its life at a moving pace.
the face of uncertainty it causes you to no longer be who you
think you are, but rather who others think you to be.
take heed young man listen. we all walk to a different tune,
abused by the nature of the world.
wishing, they call it creativity.
praying mysteriously, they call it faith, only to hope that
someone hears us. like a small whimper, a cry for help.
think of those whose request went unanswered.
in which only turned into a ghastly whisper.
your speech hushed into an unknown darkness,
as the soul fades into an unknown existence.
It's called life. A place that's only what you make it out to be.

It's all in your mind. It's all in the time.
the mental frame of what lies within the sky.
the unforeseen. the unknown. the bleakness.
I sit back and wonder.
pondering upon a moment, a moment that went by like the seconds on a clock.
my vision was steady, then my dream was shattered.
strange faces appeared, abruptly unsettling.
my sheets were dampened, my body sticky, salty to the taste. my voice was shallow. my heart raced rapidly.
a scream was hesitant. I was scared. fearful. my eyelids became a flicker as a flickering flame dancing within the night.
it's life at a moving pace. It's hate and it's love.
a place you won't know without understanding its purpose.

Written by Alphonso Luciano

Chapter 3 - Healing

3.1 Changed by Tatianna Danielle 80
3.2 Overflow by Tatianna Danielle........................ 84
3.3 Memory Lane by Tatianna Danielle.................. 85
3.4 Rest by Tatianna Danielle 86

Epiphany

* Back in the Days by Tatianna Danielle............... 87
* Back in the Days by Alphonso Luciano 89

3.5 In Memory by Alphonso Luciano...................... 91
3.6 If I Say… by Alphonso Luciano........................ 93
3.7 My Soul by Alphonso Luciano......................... 95

Healing

Healing requires you to feel emotions, to revisit pain from the inner part of your soul. To remove hurt, healing will take time. The process of healing cannot be hurried, but once exposed in time the wound will fade into a scar. The scar will tell you about your journey but should not shackle you. Free yourself and spread your wings to remove the damage caused by others and release the negative energy from paralyzing your whole being. You will be glad you did; you deserve healing. Be healed, Be free.
This is a "new beginning" for you!

—Tatianna Danielle

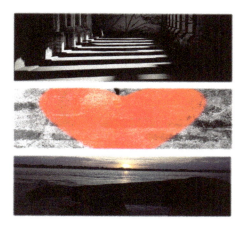

Changed

I know it is hard to see the change in me The truth is I
have spent time seeking God for the plans He has for me
And I have been made whole from the top
of my head to the souls of my feet
I am no longer lost standing in the dark,
smoke screens covering my eyes you see

I have taken off the garment of heaviness and
turned it in for the garment of praise
I forever want to declare, I will always
have the mind of Christ
The same mind that is in Christ is
in me, saying what God says
doing all that God has willed for me
to do is where I want to be

I want to vertically and horizontally always be
aligned with the will of God Being able to see
beyond the natural and enter into the supernatural
Yeah that is definitely where I want to be

I can make firm decisions because I now walk in
the image of God A new creation, disassembled
from the negativity that plagued my mind
turned my back from the lies, from the
enemy, negative words spoken over me
incidents that seeded roots of negativity in me you see

No longer bound by my past, all traumatic experiences
rejections from those close to me or abuses
that kept me from moving on
I have pleaded the blood of Jesus over my past
Now I am free to be me
To live without those shackles holding me you see

I can see clearly now the rain is gone
No longer tears flowing down so endlessly
I hold onto God's songs that whisper in my ears I
enjoy allowing God to hold me while singing and
me telling Him to never let me go Purging myself of
unforgiveness I now have unlimited forgiveness and I
love beyond the faults of others and judge no man
Being the image of God means more to me than
anything this world can ever give to me

I would rather inhale the sweetness of God's joy, peace
unlimited forgiveness and the flow of the Holy Spirit
in my life. So the change in me is real you see

I have synchronized with Christ and now
make firm decisions for my life
I have renounced the load of extra burdens, undue
stress, heaviness, unforgiveness, resentment,
bitterness, envy, or strife from laying on my chest
All hindering spirits of distraction, ungodly
attractions, confusion, delusions
and double-mindedness are removed from my life you see

My body is the temple of the Holy Ghost
I cannot be infiltrated by foreign spirits that
bring gloom to my life any longer
I disallow every trespassing thought from
entering into the gates of my soul
The generations after me will never
have to lay in this pain
Every trespassing agent assigned against my
spiritual, mental, emotional, and physical
well-being is cast out from the
perimeters of my bloodline

I have come to the realization that I am
free to be who God created me to be
I know my identity

I can breathe through whatever
persecution that comes my way
Lord your word tells me that no weapon
formed against me shall prosper in any way
Therefore, the blood of the everlasting
covenant of Jesus Christ covers me
I am no longer bound by my enemies

I understand that being changed allows me
to be who God has called me to be
Change has taken me through transitions
where the flesh did not want to enter
The Holy Spirit that lives inside of me
allowed me to be renewed and refreshed
to have reconciliation with Christ
Change has taken me to a place of serenity,
and this is where I want to be you see
Yeah being changed means everything to me

Written by Tatianna Danielle

Overflow

As I look at the clouds, I see things with so much clarity
It's like you have brought me to a place
where the clouds are even
closer to me
Much whiter and the sky has this array of light blue
There are even days when I feel like the
clouds are formed in a way just for me
And as I look to the heavens, I feel like I can
truly find you staring right back at me
Telling me a story of how my life should be
This truly is a place that brings so much peace
As I continue to take this journey,
this transition, this change
I find myself seeing life so differently
no complaining or wanting things to be my way
But I feel more of an urge to lay my plans down
in exchange for what you have for me
I'm at a place where I just want you to overflow in me
I surrender it all because you are the King!

Written by Tatianna Danielle

Memory Lane

Back down memory lane where things were better than today
looking back to when we were younger
a moment to get a glimpse of us when we were so innocent and surviving the times of the world
If we could just have the moments and the people that meant so much to us
placing a smile on our face with a gentle touch or words that would ease the day listening to grandma whistle or sing was a good day
oh, how I miss these days…

Back down memory lane where things used to be better than today
The days of sipping on sodas while taking in the sweet aroma of the outdoors, seeing the trees and beautiful grass letting the sun beam on us as we ran freely with the wind going to the candy store, sucking on a lollipop was a special treat
waiting for the mellow sound of the ice cream truck to drive through the neighborhood
oh, how these were the good days…

Memory lane is where we were able to live and not be ashamed
where we held on to the moments of love and family
taking the time to breathe with every step
not being fearful of anything
oh, how I miss these days
oh, how these were the good days…

Written by Tatianna Danielle

Rest

Life's challenges are
hitting me in my face
so real, so real
living and learning through experiences
everyday challenges
my soul needs rest, my soul needs rest
I'm coming to you, Lord
my shoulder to lean on
all I have is you
reflections of the past
emotional wreck
tears falling
I don't know what to do
when I lay my head on the pillow
I'm wrestling with thoughts in my head, in my bed
tearing me apart
I can't get no rest
exposed to things
I need peace within me
take away the hurt, Lord…I need rest
I'm screaming out your name, Lord
I'm calling on you
to take away this pain
My soul needs rest

Written by Tatianna Danielle

Back in the Days

Back in the days, when I was young
some days I reminisce about the days of wishing I could be a kid again
with my sister and brothers having a good time playing and spending time
Thinking about the times, we were innocent and fragile
Allowing the wind to take our breath away in each moment of the day
Listening to the laughter that came with the day
When we could play in the streets until the lights ended our day
even though we could not have it our way
Allowing our dreams to take us on a journey in the midst of the day
looking for love and affection at the end of the day
I always wondered why it was absent in so many of the days
we may not experience the feelings all the time
Still, these days of abandonment and rejection were standing at our door many times
Looking for ways to destroy our hearts and break us even more
No smiles when the sun shined on these days, hoping for the darkness to pass through quickly
rain poured so endlessly down our face; looking at each other thinking there has to be better days
Creating a world of interlocking hearts, allowing us to be kids every day

surviving the pain of each day, disappointments came and went throughout the day
Still looking for better days that take us back to the days

So that was a dream that played in my head as a kid

    Written by Tatianna Danielle

Back in the Days

We grew up together. More power to the people
America didn't love us, but we loved one another
From sister to brother and brother to sister
We were alone hanging on to each other
The gleam in our eyes locked at such a fragile state, we had to stick together
Our mother's struggles taught us survival
A beautiful woman but a mother that faced the world with heartache and confusion
We still had each other, left to fend for ourselves, our family was torn apart
Each one of us pulled in one direction or the other
Worn down from discouragement and broken dreams
Hope was like a feather in the wind
Like torn pages from a…no, like an unhealed wound
Tears undiscovered from a damaged heart
A box of emotions riddled with dismay
Imagine loving a woman you didn't know
Or rather looking for love in a woman who seemed not to be looking for love in her son
Yes, my mother
A person I never had a chance to call my mom
I stood alone in my mind, missing the touch of a mother, missing life as a child
Feeling strange because I knew something was missing
I would always listen but never seemed to hear her voice
It was full circle, 360 like the rotation of the earth

You look for it, but it's never there
It's never seen upon an open eye, but you know it exists
You can't touch it, but you know it's there
My mother, whom I used to call on when my dreams would turn into nightmares
When I had no understanding of where she was, my times of loneliness, waiting to be held, to be loved, to be missed
My mother, I never seemed to find her
But I knew she was there, somewhere
Just waiting to hold my hand
Waiting to hug me and tell me, "son, it's going to be okay"
The anticipation of such a day quickly faded
I grew older, my heart grew colder
My soul became chilled, I was numb and empty
I couldn't even blink a tear of sadness from my eyes, my mother
had no father, barely even a brother
I had my sisters, two of them, that secretly replaced the woman of a mother
They groomed me and taught me right along with my grandmother
Yeah, my mom's mom raised me to the best of her ability
Back in the days, we grew up together more power to the people, America didn't love us, but we loved one another

Written by Alphonso Luciano

In Memory

Turning over a new leaf.
Tryna stay afloat like a reef.
God speaking is my belief.
I cry out full of relief.
Just me and my grief.
Saddened in disbelief.
Missing everything you ever mentioned.
Feeling the tension.

In memory
suppressed by my vision.
Alternating my imagination.
The scene was vivid, picturing your image.
Coming of age, life seems staged.
My heart was caged.

In memory
of lost times, we can't get back that time.
Moments that are never taken back.
Thoughts disgruntled and packed.
Faces plastered and tacked.
Flashbacks.
Memorials and T-shirts.
Feeling hurt, emotions scorched
Unearthed like dirt.
Flourish your birth.

Seconds way too short.
Uphold the truth.

In memory.
Like a legacy.
Vacancy.
The stare in my eyes.
My soul in disguise.
I just want to run and hide.

In memory
of the memories that I find.
Behind every two words lingers a lie.
There's always a story to tell.
Despite every tale.
It's the memories in our mind we mostly fail.
…"In memory"…

Written by: Alphonso Luciano

IF I SAY...

If I say I'm sorry…
would you understand?
rather insisting we go hand to hand.
from holding hands.
until it's only one of us standing.

If I say I didn't…
would you stay or leave?
would you even believe?
stressing with no sense of relief.
Looking for healing and belief.
colorful like autumn leaves.

If I say I love you…
would you trust me?
or just look at me awkwardly?
would I be like all the others before me?
the guys that came and went from long time ago.
would it just be my ego?
with no rhyme, or reason.
or just my means to go?

If I say why…
would you respond why not?
would you even care?
when I'm never there.
and she was over here.

you were over there.
beneath the sheets.
kneeling at his feet.
and they say all men cheat.
actions repeat.
you ain't speaking.
can you feel the heat?
wake up!
I know you ain't 'sleep.

If I say…
and meant what I said.
would we still be?
would you stay or leave?
would you even believe?
would you trust me?
would you understand?
or just look at me strangely.
for the healing you need.
…"if I say"…

Written by Alphonso Luciano

My Soul

No sooner my hate begins to brew like stew over a hot
stove, after realizing the young boy
I once acknowledged no
longer appeared to be. The
jubilance that was sustained, as a
treasure of childhood instantaneously
transformed into a
darkened cloud. The skies lurid
with the flames of a burning
heart, my eyes were strained,
reflecting the truth, or rather
a story, the moist of tears simply
couldn't fade away. The
blood of one's tears is thick as syrup, a syrupy substance
that eases from my face, of a strange
place. The feel of a cold
winter leaf, or even the pebbles of
earth. Where the soul spills
from the outer shell of human eventuality. The obscurity
reveals the darkness inside. A small
cry from outside, of a fear
lurking covered with blankets in a space to hide.
My mind shattered concealed with burdens and lies.

Written by Alphonso Luciano

Chapter 4 - Love

4.1 Love Is… by Tatianna Danielle 98
4.2 Soul Mate by Tatianna Danielle 100
4.3 My Beloved by Tatianna Danielle 102
4.4 This Is Us by Tatianna Danielle 104
4.5 Love by Tatianna Danielle 105

Epiphany

* My Reflection by Tatianna Danielle 106
* My Reflection by Alphonso Luciano 109

4.6 Wonder by Alphonso Luciano 111
4.7 To Love by Alphonso Luciano 113
4.8 In Love I Thought It to Be by Alphonso Luciano 114
4.9 Loving You by Alphonso Luciano 116

Love

Love takes hold of your heart in a moment of anticipation. Before it hits the surface, it's a feeling without question. Love is something we fall into, cherish, and share—without it there is emptiness.

—Tatianna Danielle

Love Is...

Love is the soft wind that breezes by
to say hello or goodnight
Love is not crude, and was never intended to cause pain
but it is bold and beautiful in all its existence
In the midst of the day it will bring
laughter and peace to your day
Wrapping you up in the tenderness of each
touch with the words that bring safety, instead
of cause hurt to steal your innocence
Love allows you to have laughter and ask questions
whether you are young or old
in a place together or alone
it provides respect and commitment to the course of life
Love is the freshness of apologies, not insecurities
Nor regrets that ponder your mind;
however, it is dignified
as it will take you on a journey to
show you what love can be

it lingers throughout the day waiting

for someone to come its way

piercing the soul to experience the world and

touching the mere individuals seen looking

for a connection, if one will let it be

spending the time gathering memories

that will last a lifetime

Love is and will always be brought in the

pureness of family, friends, and relationships

Hopeful of a commitment with someone who will take

your breath away loving you for the rest of your days

Love is you

Love is me

Written by Tatianna Danielle

Soul Mate

Why do we bond ourselves to another? Is it the gleam in their eyes that unites to physical rapture?

The dreams shared that brings a connection to emotional bliss, gratification and pleasure are nourished by intensity and yearnings fulfilled inside.

Why do we wrap ourselves in the arms of another? Is it the security of knowing this person will be here forever?

Feels like heaven where no wrong can be seen, trusting the process and following a road of dreams and fantasies.

Bonded by like-mindedness, the freedom to be exposed and open to total trust, being my everything in the midst of storms and tribulations.

Reaching out to you in every moment to show loyalty to you forever, allowing love to be our commitment and trust to guide us through our days.

Having a long journey, where recollections of how we got here flows through our veins, every time we hear each other's name.

Smiles consume our faces when we go down memory lane, keeps us interlocked by arms, from morning to evening when the sun fades.

Reaching to you in my dreams and waking up to your sweet touch tells me you want to stay, entangled in the love we share, until the end of time.

Your love caresses me, together forever is where I want to be. You are the love of my dreams, my soul mate for eternity.

        Written by Tatianna Danielle

My Beloved

Hello darling, how are you?
I want to tell you that you are loved
I am proud of the who
you have become
Your determination really shows
through all that you do
I wish I could be there to hold you
tell you how much I cherish you
how much I love you

Beloved
I see your struggles and the mountains
that come your way
Keep smiling when the sun does not shine
when the wind takes your breath
startles you from behind or slaps you in the face
I send angels to push you through,
to cover you on every side
The strength that you display provides
for prosperity in all your days

Beloved
Keep moving in the right direction
Do not allow distractions to delay your stride
As trials and tribulations come
take time to walk with your head held high
This is only a season; it will be over in due time

Beloved
I know the difficulties of life are heavy at times
Challenges do not make your journey easy
Remember I have taught you to never give up
Through all things look up
I am here open to hold you, to catch your tears
Loving you is my greatest joy
Hey darling, you are my beloved

Written by Tatianna Danielle

This Is Us

We come from different backgrounds
With different perspectives, sometimes
our opinions cause a fuss
We have communication that attaches
our commitment and love
While other times cause our words to
never bend to let the other win
Affection that binds us through and through
It is a love that cannot be denied
We continue to stand side by side
This is us, in this together our actions bring connections
To show we will ride this out together, just the two of us
The beauty of us together is refreshing air
Not perfect, just an equivocal fraction
Connecting with another's perfectionism
establishing paths narrow and wide
to display the best of us
stronger than weak
leading each other
building an empire to have a legacy
overwhelming at times, still we seem to get by
soaring in the moments of love
trusting the process
keeping our love alive, so it never ends
this is us walking hand in hand

Written by Tatianna Danielle

Love

Do you love me, or can it be you dislike me?
I care for you, but it is hard to explain the feelings
Blocked by a wall of questions
holding me back from loving the you I see in the mirror
Blocking me from showing the care I have for you
Our love is stuck in an unknown world
One with questions of indescribable pain
Past disappointments
Abandonment that left me at the door
Should I step forward to see what this can be
Walk away to travel this road alone
Will you release me, or will I have to fight?
Discoveries and failures are a part of life
Will you take my hand and walk me through?
Will I be left standing in the room?
I want to love you and share this world
How can we move on?
Can you honestly say our love is real?

Written by Tatianna Danielle

My Reflection

My reflection of me, myself, and I tell me to love me whether anyone else does or not.
But it does question the presence every day as it wakes me up to a world of chaos and misperceptions of what I am to be.

My reflection allows me to see how the world takes every opportunity to disrespect my being by dismissing the conception of a life that was formed in the eyes of God. My beauty is questioned because it does not measure up to what you think it should be and allows for the opinions of others to say what I should look like to please the image they see. Why do you try to stagnate me with impeding thoughts that can destroy every phase of my being?

My reflection tells me if I should go or stay, so I wonder if I should step out of bed or stay and hold tight to what I have at this moment, safety and security, or greet the world with my presence, hoping to be bold and remembered as I enter each door that says hello to me.

My reflection tells me I can be whatever I want to be, while the world would beg to differ,
holding on to the past without being able to see the evolving times. With every stride there has to be determination to get by.

My reflection tells me I am not liked in these streets. Could it be the way I command the room or the confidence that is seen?

Was it all the degrees that you thought weren't for me? Yes, I spent many hours making sure I was equipped to speak eloquently to the elite. No, I am not ghetto or a thug walking the streets; did you know that doesn't even connect to me?

My reflection tells me to not settle for the lies and deceit that you bring. I am more than able to make decisions that will provide for me. So, no thank you to blocking my path of being where you are. I will get there in time with dignity and respect being on my side.

My reflection tells me everything I need to know about who I am and what I want to be in this world. When you see me know that I continually love despite the barriers that you put up for me.

My reflection tells me what you will not say to me, so you can be oblivious to the chatting in the streets to mute my voice or tear me down so I will not have the strength to make it in this world.

Remember through the journey of life obstacles will come, but when someone walks a world of displeasures, love will guide and embrace the whole being, giving consent for me to do anything.

Written by Tatianna Danielle

My Reflection

I stand there looking at it.
It's me, myself, and I.
In the mirror my reflection
glances back at me,
displaying my inner self,
the most high of
myself; it's me.
I'm noticing everything,
everything others see in me,
everything I don't
see in myself.
I am a reflection,
a reflection of every action
of those around me,
even those who
whisper about me.
I know they see me; it's me,
a split image of
those before me.
they can either hate me
or understand me.
my reflection,
it's all in the mind,
a man reflecting
on his word,
a man reflecting on
his sole intentions.

We all reflect on
someone, somewhere.
You can even reflect on
yourself going nowhere.
It's all in your reflection,
how you choose to see it.
Your reflection—what's
staring back at you
It's like an illusion.
Life is reflected off the
waters of the earth.
What do you see?
Who is it that you see?
It's a glimpse of your flaws,
a sense of your
expectations.
It's the universal law,
reflection, complication,
and resolution.
It's a time span, a
repeat of history,
tales like a real story.
a reflection of lies
and truth,
reflected and told
like a true story.

Sometimes you can smile
but often your reflection
won't smile back.
It's grim—a shadow—dark.
Its unforbidden.
It's my reflection.

It's a binding image.
It's character.
It's whatever you want it
to be. It's you, defined by
you, honored by you.

Written by Alphonso Luciano

WONDER

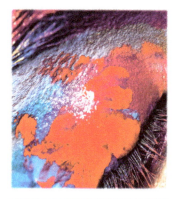

I WONDER, I wonder as my hand graces this page, does your mind envision me, even if it's just a mere image of my smile, or the sound of my joyful laughter?

I WONDER, I wonder if you think about me as the sun elapses from the moon or when the melodies play a soft tune, through the night as a whisper…

I WONDER, I wonder if your memories consist of the times I looked into your eyes, captivated by your beauty through the rays of the sun, such as the skies to the stars…

I WONDER, I wonder if my thoughts may be whirling too fast, or if my words might be exceedingly emotional…

I Wonder, I wonder with this time apart, did I grow fonder in your heart? I wonder if I'm missed as the years I have missed. The opportunities that passed and the features of my daughter that seem to be obsolete, within a world cold and confused…

I Wonder, I wonder at this very moment what's on your mind. May a tear spill from your eye and fall unto the hand of the Lord. He'll land your love upon the cushion of my soul, rendering of pain and resentment until we meet again…

"I Wonder."

    Written by Alphonso Luciano

TO LOVE

To love you ultimately, love is like no other.
undoubtedly is to be blinded by your
magnitude; your beatitude.
is all a result of your gratitude
magnificently is to love you dearly, fairly.
in the wind my heart wears thin.
complications within. Now and then gambling to win.
to love is never no end. Feelings invested
and ingested thru the smog.
A cloudy fog of a hazy remembrance, yet
a firm stance stuck in a trance.
My thoughts unsettling drawing a blank.
Unnervingly to love like the brilliance from above.
The tenderness of a dove is the push of a shove.
To rain droplets of joy to the warmth of
moments to enjoy makes my insides coy.
A hug or just a kiss. A sense of full bliss.
And it's you that I miss. Sparks of a smile felt from a mile
Feeling like I'm exiled from existence.
This is my sentence for instance.
I love to love you even when I'm down and blue.
This is forever true, in my mind without a clue.
Sick like the flu.
to live without you.
to know is to love.
and to love is to know.
…"To Love"…

Written by Alphonso Luciano

In Love I Thought It to Be

I was told one day that it would be days like this.
Days where I would find myself alone and afraid.
Afraid of the day that you would leave me.
Deviant of everything you told me.
Pushing me, rather than pulling me.

"In love I thought it to be…"
Love sustaining multiple colors.
Love in all its entirety.
Love caused me to grasp your soul.
I stare vacantly into your eyes.
Fondling your hips.
I urge you closer.
Love urges me further.
Yet I stop stepping away from your temptation.
Falling in love implies a loss of balance.
Real love is different from that disorienting infatuation.
True love provides foundation.
It strengthens and builds you.

"In love I thought it to be…"
Love is a reflection of one another.
Love is described by four simple letters.
Defined by a feeling of loyalty.
Love was always like the heavens in the sky.
Always there even when we least expect it to be.
"In love I thought it to be…"

Love to endure.
Love to match your expression with the words of your heart.
Affection is from the very start.
The beginning sealed by the faith of my love.
With the beauty of a dove.
The scattered clouds from above.
Raindrops shower my crown.
Pellets trickle down the side of my face.
Life flashes before my eyes.
Love subsides within my mind.

"In love I thought it to be…"
Dancing above the stars.
Singing my name like a twinkling star.
It was love from afar.
My thoughts expressed, my ideas transcended into a poem.
"In love I thought it to be."

Written by Alphonso Luciano

Loving You

I love you now.

I love you tomorrow.

I love you beyond the days.

beyond the moon and back again.

I love you over and over again.

I love your beauty.

I love your personality.

the means of prosperity.

to define perfection.

dedication is what defines us.

our loyalty and equality.

I love you.

I love your strive,

your devotion and inspiration.

loving you is like loving a nation.

my everything is everything I see in you.

it is everything I never seen in myself.

I love you for loving and trusting me.

when I didn't trust myself.

to uplift me.

when the weight seemed too heavy.

my heart was broken like a levee.

my emotions swayed and wavy.

look at what love made me.

wild and crazy.

this was different.

being in love.

you were very different.

in love with you.

before the syllables left my lips.

look at this it was such a perfect fit.

we were hitched in bliss.

from our very first touch it was a wish

a dream that became reality.

Loving you.

Written by: Alphonso Luciano

Chapter 5 - Peace

5.1 Misunderstood by Tatianna Danielle............ 120

5.2 My Heart by Tatianna Danielle...................... 122

5.3 Forgiveness by Tatianna Danielle 124

Epiphany

* Our Peace by Tatianna Danielle and
Alphonso Luciano... 126

5.4 My ol' earth by Alphonso Luciano 129

5.5 One Day by Alphonso Luciano........................ 131

5.6 Moment by Alphonso Luciano........................ 134

PEACE

*Peace is music to my soul and calming to my whole
being—a journey always beautiful, and a
voice never heard. Breathe and listen
to the inner peace within;
you will find understanding and peace in your heart.*

—Tatianna Danielle

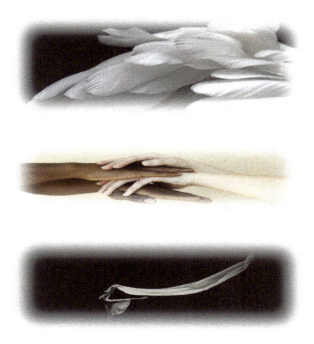

Misunderstood

When you look at me
You automatically judge me
As a person who is not fit
to sit with your kind
You say words that are unkind

Misunderstood
Misunderstood for the
color of my skin
Misunderstood for the
clothes that I wear
Misunderstood for the
way that I walk
Misunderstood for the
way that I talk

Misunderstood
When I am silent
You find a way to paint
a picture of darkness
Changing my character
so far from who I am
Have you ever thought about
the road I have walked?
Did you ever wonder to
ask are you okay?

Misunderstood
For wanting to be creative and have free expression
To stand in a space alone has you
wondering if I will ever make it
Do you wonder why there is silence every
time you come around where I stand?
Do you ask yourself why there is distance between
how you identify me to my true being?

Misunderstood
I don't even know why all these
opinions of me play in my head
Why do I care what has been said?
Questioning the unforeseen
scared of one abandoning me

Misunderstood
Did you know that trust is an issue for me?
Did you know that I want to pull this wall
down and allow you into my world?
Still I am trying to breathe through
hurt and traumatic experiences
Every day putting pieces of life together
Removing the struggles as much as possible
So I can live a life of happiness
A life of freedom
To breathe without fear
Misunderstood

Written by Tatianna Danielle

My Heart

Follow your heart is what people say
But never did they say one day it could be broken
I gave you my heart and you should have
taken it and safeguarded it from pain
However, you used it and abused it for selfish gain
Returned it broken—in pieces, shattered
even more by a mere touch
Tears fall due to the damage caused
Every tear that falls down searches for
the path of love to bring healing
but life seems so bleak
Deep within my heart, I am hurting so much
My heart is not to be broken, neither is my soul
What my heart needs is a calming touch
The only peace I see is standing in
the sheerness of the cold
A connection to an atmosphere that
brings peace to my soul
Given the opportunity to freely be who I am to be

Allowing my heart to breathe, sing, and move
without confirmation from you to do so
As the pieces of my heart are gathered,
I will walk through healing
Not allowing your recklessness to
stop me from loving myself
I will safeguard it from any pain familiar to you
I will blossom, I will be
surrounded by the beauty of the earth
sounds of nature making a connection to my soul
trees blowing in a synchronized posture to welcome
my heart to heal, to breathe
My heart is precious, and it shall have peace

Written by Tatianna Danielle

Forgiveness

I see the mistreatment you bring
And I wonder why you continue to do this to me
So angry with all your expressions
Your actions show inconsistencies that don't make sense
Your words cut like a knife, without empathy for anything

Being apologetic is just a routine to get you through the night
Then the next day a circle of your egotistical ways
Bring you back to outbursts that expose your pain
How the guilt and shame cause you to blame others for the things you've seen
But they are not connected to me

I wasn't the one to hurt you
Nor the one who deserves to allow your pride
To destroy the relationship you have with me
Take a minute to stop and breathe

Release past pains to keep them from scarring the
The person who stands beside you every day
Remember forgiveness is a choice that only you can decide
When the world shows disappointments, you have to look up to the sky
And remember forgiveness is necessary to get you by

I realize forgiveness will take you from holding onto violations by others
Heal from the verbal and physical abuse projected
Have the freedom to not be shackled to the bad memories and flashbacks
Disturbed sleep that brings chaos to your days
But wake up to refreshing days where mistreatment is released by making a sound decision to not allow it to be
Attached to me

I know that you do not control my destiny
Learning that you cannot affect me with your ways
Growing stronger every day
I can embrace the wind in the day and storms that arrive at night
Through knowing forgiveness is my everything and is what gets me by
Forgiveness provides serenity to carry me

Written by Tatianna Danielle

Our Peace

It is hard to define peace of another; it is different for everyone
You have to go through the process to understand what disrupted your being and made you uneasy in times that brought unpleasure.

Peace is a decision that has to be made, in the reminiscence of it all
someone is to blame for the disruptions that cause these uneasy thoughts that change the direction of your day.

Still you can breathe in the freshness of each day
have control of how you will end your day. The glimpse of the pureness of the air will guide you in all your endeavors to block the pain.

Allow peace to hold you and wrap you in the place you find pureness and light
Giving you that moment which allows you to stand without worry, no judgment
And the care is all about you being seen as a human being; such a nice place to be

Take a moment to feel the atmosphere to find your peace
Your peace is the most important place, not too many people should wonder
To sit at your table the heart has to grow fonder
Connecting to the inner being of a person, instead of the outer appearance
This is a secret place to enhance your being.

Take a moment to feel the atmosphere to find your peace
spiritual meditation is the pathway to all things to come
its mystic energy reaches from error to truth from pain to peace
it will become incorporated into your very being.

Centered upon divine realities is the very essence of the soul
the means of shaking off darkness of ignorance a story that was never told
unfold the purity of power which is led by the profound peace
to grow within mind, body, and soul through thought the truth is perceived.

Uphold from beyond vividly representing your imagination to arouse a deep compassion
for those with no aspiration with absolute meekness, practicing being fearless
great will be your bliss to be one with your peace
old things will pass on, and all things become new
time will cease no more anxiety and sorrow

to be established in the unchangeable a world of peace dwell in the very heart unto the beginning where everything starts.

Written by Tatianna Danielle and Alphonso Luciano

My ol' earth

360 degrees of completion
the truth, she is not swayed negatively with emotion
yet uses her emotion to continue to propel her towards the truth
the earth is humble, yet firm, flexible, but not weak
confident, but not cocky
she is a student and a teacher, reaching beyond the means of her expectations
the mother earth is what she is referred to, the mother of all mothers
but it's not the land that's cast upon men nor the green of grass that blankets our fields of vegetation

she is constantly aspiring to gain wisdom, so she learns through trial and error
taking the best part of every situation
placing value on the jewels she has received
she is a mother, a childbearing woman
the earth, her energy is always in motion
her skin smooth to the touch
her voice is full of clarity
she is a mother, a mother of strength
she strives for greatness
the earth is productive, she builds diligently, she never comes empty-handed

even if it is simply lending a helping hand
time reflects on the past, but time moves us forward, and the things we wish we could take back; relived and memorized
it's all stuck in the past, stuck in a moment
seeping from the pores of those who seek the heap of love
the embracement of faith and the feel of trust
the eye of her, the mother of wisdom
the life of knowledge, the fear of understanding
a soft whisper from the lips of a woman I never met, an image I've only seen in
photographs, a picture painted in my mind, created only by my imagination

Written by Alphonso Luciano

One Day

I will be set free.

I will be able to breathe and walk amongst the trees.

seeing the colorful sight of leaves

right there in front of me.

the city aroma will take my breath away.

it will awaken me from feeling like I was in a coma.

with the years past there may be a gloss in my eye.

shared by a blurry vision.

smudged like glass.

Still my unearthed senses will come alive

seconds gone for way too long where minutes stalled.

erasing the past, allowing the baggage

to be tugged and hauled

memories failed my mind of the past, I

have sailed to a higher level of peace

onto another realm of life where I can spread my wings.

No more being shackled to this world,

pain disturbing my sleep

I am set free from the bondage others have instilled in me

even when I don't understand another wave
may try to make me misbehave.
Corruption does not live here with me
I hold on to the peace received and breath
in every moment of being free
one day is all I could ever say.
my emotions and confusion won't plague me
congested like a vessel of my heart being tugged
such a hassle to be stuck in time
loss of energy but peace will be mine
I think from the beginning and on again.
for everything that's lost is someone else's gain.
to the unknown and what's shown.
You'll never know until one day just as
yesterday that's all I could say.
"One day."

Written by Alphonso Luciano

Moment

Can I just get a moment
To say something, I need to say
Let me gather my thoughts in order
To tell y'all something that's on my heart today
I want to embrace this moment to allow my voice to be heard
Although my heart is racing.
Slightly nervous and disturbed.
I just need a moment, a moment to control my breathing.
This is heavy, just to say…
The timing just isn't right.
My mind isn't shining too bright.
Don't shut down on me right now.
Not here at this moment.
I want to say what I need to say.
Now I can't seem to find the words.
To express my gratitude
I'm stuck standing here.
All my people facing me.
My mouth agape, but nothing is coming out.
I just want to shout.
I just need a moment.
To better prepare myself.
I wonder if it's too late.
I'm thinking of things that don't even relate.
Intensely they are awaiting.
Anticipating, I'm stalled.
I could've just called.

Embarrassed and frightened.
I'm fighting the urge to cry.
I'm trying to spill out these words.
I should've just walked away.
Instead I decided to stay.
I'm tired of hiding.
Such a finding.
This is me!
And what it's going to be.
I just need a moment.
I lost track of time.
I was supposed to be elsewhere.
But I'm here.
Still haven't said nothing.
My knees are shaking.
I feel hot like I'm baking.
These clothes are smothering me, just suffocating me.
I cleared my throat, maybe I'm just thirsty.
I should've thought of that first.
This isn't going as planned.
Excuse me, please.
I just need a moment; I realize I don't have peace

Written by: Alphonso Luciano

About the Author

Tatianna Danielle and Alphonso Luciano are two individuals who were born and raised in Ohio. They grew up reading the dictionary and encyclopedia to explore words and build their vocabulary, which was influenced by both their grandmother and Tatianna's father, to build their repertoire for life. The discovery of words connected them both to have a desire for writing around the age of six years old. From childhood to adulthood, both created a collection of poetry. Revisiting their art brought moments of reflection that allowed them to share their poetry and create relatable topics. To their surprise, both experienced epiphanies. Although these poets live in different parts of the world, Tatianna Danielle and Alphonso Luciano's collaboration brings their work of art into two different writing styles, which complement each other very well. The emotions are real, painted with many awes. The poets' first collection of poetry together is *Epiphany*.

When not writing poetry, you can find both poets enjoying the simplicity of life such as listening to various genres of music, exploring art, and reading works done by other poets and authors. Tatianna has a Bachelor of Arts degree in Applied Behavioral Science and Sociology and continuing her education by pursuing a Master of Science degree in Human and Social Services. She enjoys helping others and spending time participating in different community projects. She is a tea enthusiast, which allows her many opportunities to enjoy a nice cup tea throughout the day while also researching its health benefits to share with others. Alphonso is taking classes in business management. He loves helping others build their business, working out and being creative; spending time drawing and writing for other projects is his greatest joy.

CPSIA information can be obtained
at www.ICGtesting.com
Printed in the USA
BVHW060201130822
644454BV00010B/572